Marvelous Norwegian Recipes

An Illustrated Cookbook of Scandinavian Dish Ideas!

BY: Allie Allen

COOK & ENJOY

Copyright 2020 Allie Allen

Copyright Notes

This book is written as an informational tool. While the author has taken every precaution to ensure the accuracy of the information provided therein, the reader is warned that they assume all risk when following the content. The author will not be held responsible for any damages that may occur as a result of the readers' actions.

The author does not give permission to reproduce this book in any form, including but not limited to: print, social media posts, electronic copies or photocopies, unless permission is expressly given in writing.

Table of Contents

Introduction 6

Norwegian breakfasts are filling and hearty. Try one soon… 8

   1 – Lemon Curd Pancakes 9

   2 – Norwegian Porridge & Cranberries 12

   3 – Salmon & Egg Sandwich 14

   4 – Norwegian Waffles 16

   5 – Norwegian Torsk 18

   6 – Crab Salad 20

   7 – Norwegian Lefsa 22

   8 – Roasted Halibut 24

   9 – Bjarne Meatballs 27

   10 – Norwegian Fish Cakes 30

   11 – Ovnskokt Kveite 32

   12 – Norway Cabbage Rolls 35

   13 – Norwegian Ribbe 38

   14 – Snarol Drink 40

15 – Beef & Cabbage 42

16 – Trout in Paper Wrappers 44

17 – Salmon & Matcha Spice 46

18 – Baked Fish with Macaroni 49

19 – Norwegian Curried Lamb 52

20 – Norwegian Lemon Chicken 54

21 – Norwegian Saffron Salmon 56

22 – Norway Salmon Chowder 59

23 – Norwegian Spinach & Quinoa Salad 62

24 – Stewed Peas 64

25 – Norwegian Leeks & Tuna Pasta 66

Norway is home to a diverse array of dessert choices. Try one of these wonderful desserts soon…
.... 68

26 – Rice & Date Pudding 69

27 – Cinnamon Thumbs 71

28 – Norwegian Spiced Krumkake 73

29 – Norwegian Apple Cake 75

30 – Kringla Cookies 78

Conclusion 80

About the Author 81

Author's Afterthoughts 83

Introduction

How can you integrate Norwegian foods into your recipe repertoire at home?

Can you seek out the different ingredients you'll need to make these dishes?

Are you curious about the various ways in which Nordic foods can make your recipes tastier?

Norway has among the longest coastlines in the world, and that means plenty of fresh seafood. The fjords, with their clear, cold water, are home to many fish. Preparing fish is a vital part of Norwegian cooking.

Many fresh ingredients are used in most Norwegian kitchens, and they prepare multitudes of meals from scratch. Their local brewers of coffee have reinvented the love of coffee in Norway, and international awards tell you they're on the right track.

In the early 20th century, the standard of living in Norway was somewhat poor. Many people ate porridge for two or more meals per day. They could barely grow enough food to feed everyone. But wealth arrived within the last 125 years or so, and with it came more diverse dishes.

Norwegians enjoy cooking with apples and berries, which grow nicely in the country's warm days, which are pleasant but not plentiful. Wild mushrooms and other vegetables find their way into tasty dishes, with rich aromas. The seasonings utilized in Norway, like caraway seed and dill, add savory flavors to the fish and game used so well. Try a true Norwegian recipe soon…

Norwegian breakfasts are filling and hearty. Try one soon...

1 – Lemon Curd Pancakes

These mini pancakes are golden brown and puffy, perfect for breakfast. You could serve them for a dessert, too. In this recipe, they are filled with prepared lemon curd & blueberries.

Makes 2-4 Servings

Cooking + Prep Time: 35 minutes

Ingredients:

- 3 eggs, medium
- 1/2 cup of flour, all-purpose
- 1/2 cup of milk, whole
- 1 tbsp. of sugar, granulated
- 1 tsp. of vanilla extract, pure
- 2 tsp. of lemon zest, grated finely
- 1 pinch of salt, kosher
- 4 tbsp. of butter, unsalted

Optional: sugar, powdered, to dust

For the filling

- 1/4 cup of lemon curd, prepared
- 1/2 pint of blueberries, fresh

Instructions:

1. Preheat the oven to 425F.

2. Add the milk, flour, eggs, vanilla, sugar, lemon zest and salt together in food processor. Blend till you have a smooth texture.

3. Add butter to two heavy, oven-safe skillets. Place in oven till butter melts, several minutes. Pour 1/2 batter in each skillet. Return to oven. Bake for 18-20 minutes, till pancakes are golden and puffed. Reduce temperature of oven to 300F. Bake for five more minutes.

4. Remove the pancakes from your oven. Serve with lemon curd, blueberries and powdered sugar, if desired.

2 – Norwegian Porridge & Cranberries

This is a wonderful treat for breakfast, and simple to make. It's sweet and salty at the same time. Serve it with cranberries and cinnamon on the top.

Makes 3 Servings

Cooking + Prep Time: 70 minutes

Ingredients:

- 3/4 cup of rice, medium-grain, white
- 1 & 1/2 cups of water, filtered
- 2 & 1/2 cups of milk, 1%
- 1 tbsp. of butter, unsalted
- 1 tbsp. of honey, pure
- 1 tbsp. of sugar, granulated
- 1 tsp. of salt, kosher
- 2 tsp. of vanilla extract, pure

To top: powdered cinnamon, butter, dried cranberries

Instructions:

1. In med. pot, add water and rice. Bring to boil. Lower the heat to simmer. Cover pot and set for 10 minutes, till rice absorbs all water.

2. Add 1/3 milk, then stir and cover. Leave till consistency has thickened. Add a bit more milk each time the consistency of the porridge thickens. Repeat till you have used all the milk. Porridge should be thick, and rice should be tender.

3. Add honey, butter, salt, vanilla extract and sugar. Stir thoroughly.

4. Turn off heat. Pour porridge into bowls. Top with small butter pats, if using, a bit of powdered cinnamon and the dried cranberries. Serve.

3 – Salmon & Egg Sandwich

Smoked salmon and eggs create a taste sensation when they're served together for breakfast. You can use any kind of bread you prefer.

Makes 6 Servings

Cooking + Prep Time: 15 minutes

Ingredients:

- 4 oz. of salmon, smoked
- 4 eggs, large
- 1/4 tsp. of salt, kosher
- 1/4 tsp. of pepper, ground
- 2 sprigs of fresh dill
- 2 tsp. of butter, soft
- 12 slices of mini rye party bread, or your preferred bread

Instructions:

1. Butter bread. Set it aside.

2. Flake the fish.

3. Scramble the eggs with kosher salt & ground pepper in large curds till barely done. Eggs should be creamy, rather than dry.

4. Place the eggs on slices of bread. Top with the salmon. Sprinkle with the dill. Serve.

4 – Norwegian Waffles

This is a traditional Norwegian breakfast which is usually cooked there by Norwegian waffle irons. You can use whatever type of waffle iron you already have – yours just might be a bit thicker.

Makes 2-4 Servings

Cooking + Prep Time: 40 minutes

Ingredients:

- 4 eggs, large
- 1/2 cup of sugar, granulated
- 1 cup of milk, 2%
- 1 cup of sour cream, reduced fat
- 2 cups of flour, all-purpose
- 2 tsp. of baking powder, low sodium
- 1 stick of melted butter, unsalted
- 1/2 tsp. of cinnamon, ground

Instructions:

1. Heat waffle iron.

2. Crack eggs into medium bowl. Add sugar, then whisk them together.

3. Add sour cream and milk. Whisk again and combine well.

4. Add flour, cinnamon and baking soda. Gently mix.

5. Add melted butter. Mix again. Pour the batter into your waffle iron. Cook for three to four minutes, till timer goes off and waffles are golden brown. Serve.

Norway is famous for many of their lunch and dinner recipes. They also have some delicious side dishes and appetizers…

5 – Norwegian Torsk

This dish is made simply with broiled & buttered cod fish fillets. The recipe here utilizes frozen fish, and you don't need to defrost them before using them.

Makes 6 Servings

Cooking + Prep Time: 35 minutes

Ingredients:

- 6 x 6-oz. cod fillets
- 6 cups of water, filtered
- 1 cup of sugar, white
- 2 tbsp. of salt, kosher
- 1 & 1/2 cups of melted butter, unsalted
- A dash of paprika

Instructions:

1. Preheat the broiler and grease a baking sheet lightly.

2. Place fish in large sized pan. Mix water, salt and sugar together. Pour water mixture on top of fish, covering it fully. Add additional water if needed. Bring water to boil on med-high and boil for three to five minutes.

3. Remove fish from the water. Blot on some paper towels, removing excess water from fish. Brush with six tbsp. of melted butter. Use paprika to sprinkle.

4. Broil for eight to 10 minutes per 1" thickness till fillets are a golden brown color. Serve with the rest of the butter.

6 – Crab Salad

If you've had crab salad from Norway, you may have fallen in love with it quite easily. The crab meat in Norway is always fresh, and that **Makes** the salad so much better.

Makes 6 Servings

Cooking + Prep Time: 40 minutes

Ingredients:

- 10 & 1/2 ounces of shredded crab meat, white (imitation is ok, too)
- 1 cup of mayonnaise, light
- 2 tbsp. of chopped chives
- 2 tbsp. of chopped dill
- 2 tbsp. of chopped parsley
- 2 tbsp. of fresh-squeezed lemon juice
- 1 can of drained, washed chickpeas
- 1 chopped bell pepper, red
- Salt, kosher
- Pepper, WHITE, as desired

Instructions:

1. Add crab meat, mayo, chives, lemon juice and dill together in large-sized bowl. Fold, rather than mixing.

2. Add and mix in bell peppers and chickpeas.

3. Allow salad to chill for 1/2 hour before you serve on lettuce leaves or bread.

7 – Norwegian Lefsa

These potato-based pancakes or crepe-style lefsa are often served for holiday meals, but you can enjoy them anytime. Be sure the dough balls remain cold till you roll them out.

Makes 8 Servings

Cooking + Prep Time: 55 minutes + 8 hours refrigeration time

Ingredients:

- 18 scrubbed baking potatoes, medium
- 1/2 cup of whipping cream, heavy
- 1/2 cup of butter, unsalted
- 1 tbsp. of salt, kosher
- 1 tbsp. of sugar, white
- 4 cups of flour, all-purpose

Instructions:

1. Peel the potatoes. Place them all in large-sized pot with water to cover + extra. Bring to boil. Allow potatoes to boil till they soften. Drain them and mash them well.

2. In large bowl, combine eight cups of mashed potatoes with cream, butter, sugar and salt. Cover potatoes. Refrigerate them overnight.

3. Mix flour into mashed potatoes. Roll into tennis-ball sized orbs. Keep the dough balls in refrigerator.

4. Remove one ball at a time from refrigerator. Roll them out on floured work surface.

5. Fry lefsa in grill. Place on dish towel after cooking. Fold a towel over them to maintain their warmth. Stack the lefsa in a loose pile. Keep them covered so they don't dry out until you serve.

8 – Roasted Halibut

This is a healthy dish that also delivers bright flavors and colors to your dinner. Halibut and other white fish come out juicy and tender when you roast them.

Makes 5 Servings

Cooking + Prep Time: 55 minutes

Ingredients:

- 1 & 1/3 pounds of plum tomatoes, ripe
- 2 cloves of peeled, smashed garlic
- 1/3 cup of wine, white
- 1 to 2 tbsp. of tomato paste
- Salt, kosher, as desired
- Pepper, ground, as desired
- 1 & 1/2 lbs. of halibut fillet
- 2 seeded, sliced bell peppers
- 1 handful olives
- 2 tbsp. of drained capers
- 1 tsp. of fennel seeds
- 1 wedge-cut lemon
- 1 tbsp. of butter, unsalted

For garnishing: olive oil, 1 handful chopped parsley & thinly sliced slivers of red onions

Instructions:

1. Preheat the oven to 350 degrees F.

2. Rinse, then chop tomatoes in large chunks. Place in food processor. Add garlic. Process till pureed, allowing for some texture (not ultra-smooth).

3. Put tomatoes in skillet. Bring to boil. Turn heat down to med. Add tomato paste and wine. Cook for 13-15 minutes or so at gentle bubble, allowing it to thicken. Season as desired.

4. Pour sauce in bottom of baking pan. Top with fish. Add peppers, capers, olives, lemon wedges and fennel seeds around fish. Nestle all into sauce.

5. Dot fish using butter. Cover loosely with aluminum foil. Bake for 35-40 minutes. Remove foil after 20 minutes. Finish dish under broiler to add color.

6. Top fish with onions and parsley. Use oil to drizzle and sprinkle with pepper. Serve.

9 – Bjarne Meatballs

These are not your typical Norwegian meatballs. A Norwegian man perfected them and he eventually became a professional chef. They're quite unique.

Makes 12 Servings

Cooking + Prep Time: 1 & 1/2 hour

Ingredients:

For the meatballs

- 1/2 cup of milk, 2%
- 3/4 cup of breadcrumbs, plain
- 2 eggs, large
- 1 grated onion, large
- 1 tbsp. of fresh ginger, grated
- 1 tbsp. of salt, kosher
- 2 tsp. of nutmeg, ground

Optional: 2 tsp. of garlic, minced

- 1 & 1/2 tsp. of black pepper, ground
- 3 lbs. of ground beef, 85% lean

For the gravy

- 4 cups of broth, beef
- 3 tbsp. of butter, unsalted
- 2 tbsp. of onion, minced
- 5 tbsp. of flour, all-purpose
- 1/2 cup of cream, heavy
- A dash of pepper, cayenne
- A dash of pepper, WHITE

Instructions:

1. Preheat oven to 400F. Grease jelly roll pan.

2. Combine the milk, breadcrumbs, onion, eggs, salt, ginger, garlic, nutmeg & ground pepper in medium bowl. Allow to stand till breadcrumbs have absorbed milk, five minutes or so. Stir till barely mixed. Add beef. Mix till blended well. Shape into 1" balls. Place on pan prepared above.

3. Bake in 400F oven till browned, 15-18 minutes and set the meatballs aside.

4. Melt the butter in large-sized skillet on med-high. Sauté the onion till tender, three minutes or so. Add and stir flour. Cook till browned lightly, two minutes or so.

5. Add the broth slowly. Stir while cooking gravy till thickened and smooth. Blend in the cream, ground pepper and cayenne pepper.

6. Stir cooked meatballs gently into the gravy. Heat them through. Don't allow them to boil, though. Serve.

10 – Norwegian Fish Cakes

These fish cakes are sold in cafes and made to sell at some supermarkets. They taste even better when you make them yourself.

Makes 6 Servings

Cooking + Prep Time: 1 hour & 10 minutes

Ingredients:

- 1 pound of fillets, whitefish – haddock or cod are fine
- 1/2 tsp. of salt, kosher
- 1/8 tsp. of pepper, ground
- 1/8 tsp. of nutmeg, ground
- 1 white from large egg
- 1 & 1/2 tbsp. of cornstarch
- 1/2 to 1 cup of milk, ice-cold + extra as needed

To fry: 1 to 2 tbsp. of oil, canola

Instructions:

1. Pat fillets of whitefish dry using paper towels. Slice them into chunks. Grind the chunks in your food processor.

2. Add kosher salt, ground pepper, egg white, nutmeg and cornstarch. Process till blended well. Then, turn food processor to low speed and pour milk portion through chute slowly. Continue to add milk till mixture has texture like moist paste. Place mixture into bowl.

3. Heat the oil in large-sized pan over med. heat. Form mixture into balls, then slightly flatten them. Add to pan. Fry cakes till they are golden brown and serve.

11 – Ovnskokt Kveite

This fish dinner is especially delicious when you serve it over rice with green beans and toast. Following the recipe virtually guarantees an unforgettably wonderful meal.

Makes 6 Servings

Cooking + Prep Time: 1 hour & 35 minutes

Ingredients:

- 2 lbs. of halibut fresh, de-skinned & boned – reserve the skin and bones
- 2 cups of water, filtered
- 2 tbsp. of flour, all-purpose
- 1 tbsp. of lemon juice, fresh
- 1/2 cup of butter, unsalted
- 1/2 tsp. of pepper, ground
- 1 tsp. of salt, kosher
- 2 tbsp. of sherry
- 1/2 cup of cream, light
- 2 yolks from large eggs

Instructions:

1. Place fish bones and skin in pan with water. Bring to boil. Reduce by 1/4. Strain. Reserve 1 & 1/2 cups.

2. Preheat oven to 400F.

3. Cut halibut in bite-sized pieces. Coat them with flour. Heat the butter in skillet on med-high. Fry halibut till barely golden brown in color. Transfer to baking dish and arrange in one layer. Sprinkle with the lemon juice. Season as desired.

4. Pour the fish stock into pan where you fried fish. Cook on med. heat for three to five minutes. Stir and scrape bottom of pan. Add and stir in the sherry and cream. Continue to cook for five more minutes.

5. Whisk egg yolks in small sized bowl till they are frothy. Whisk in small amount of cream sauce slowly. Whisk mixture into sauce. Pour it over the fish in your baking dish. Bake in 400F oven for 25-30 minutes and serve.

12 – Norway Cabbage Rolls

I was never a big eater of cabbage rolls until I tried this recipe. They are a real crowd-pleaser for appetizers or dinners.

Makes 4-6 Servings

Cooking + Prep Time: 1 hour & 15 minutes

Ingredients:

- 2 cabbage heads, medium
- 4 cups of water, to boil leaves of cabbage
- Salt, kosher
- 1/2 pound of beef, ground
- 1 & 1/2 tsp. of salt, kosher
- 1/4 tsp. of pepper, ground
- 1/4 tsp. of ground nutmeg
- 1/4 tsp. of ground ginger
- 1 egg, medium
- 2 tbsp. of cream, heavy
- 1 can of tomatoes, crushed
- Salt, kosher
- Pepper, ground

Instructions:

1. Bring large sized pot of water to boil. Add 1 tbsp. salt. Add one cabbage head. Allow to boil for five to seven minutes, till outer layers are beginning to appear transparent.

2. Remove cabbage head from water. Allow to cool off on baking sheet till it has cooled enough that you can handle it. Repeat same process on each cabbage head.

3. Once cabbage is cool enough to touch, remove leaves from core. They should be malleable and flexible.

4. To make filling, add beef, spices, salt, cream and egg in bowl. Combine ingredients till incorporated well.

5. Add lump of the filling in middle of cabbage leaf. Wrap leaf edges around meat, forming parcel. Repeat process till you use all leaves and meat.

6. Place cabbage parcels in baking dish. Pour tomatoes over top and season as desired. Lastly, bake in 375F oven for 35 to 40 minutes, till tomatoes bubble and thicken into sauce. Serve warm.

13 – Norwegian Ribbe

Many people in Norway serve Ribbe for dinner on Christmas eve. It's easy to make anytime, and you can even make it a day ahead if you like.

Makes Various # of Servings

Cooking + Prep Time: 3 hours & 25 minutes + 1-day marinating time

Ingredients:

- 6 & 1/2 pounds of skin-on pork belly ribs
- 4 & 1/2 tsp. of salt, kosher
- 3 tsp. of pepper, ground
- 10 fluid oz. of water, filtered

Instructions:

1. Cut pork ribs on skin and make many shallow-depth incisions.

2. Sprinkle meat with kosher salt & ground pepper. Place in the refrigerator for one day so it becomes soaked well.

3. Remove meat from refrigerator and place with skin side facing up on the grill grate. Pour water at bottom of form. Wrap form in aluminum foil. Place in 450F oven. Bake for 45 to 50 minutes.

4. Remove foil and lower oven temperature to 225F. Bake meat for two more hours till it's tender.

5. If the skin is crispy and meat is flowing white juice from incisions, it's ready. Remove from oven and garnish as desired. Serve.

14 – Snarol Drink

Quick beer is a party favorite in Norway. It's not an alcoholic drink. It's made with any brand of malt drink that is alcohol-free.

Makes 3 liters

Cooking + Prep Time: 20 minutes

Ingredients:

- 100 fluid oz. of water, filtered
- 8 & 3/4 oz. of sugar, granulated
- 1/2 fresh lemon, juice only
- 1 cup of vørterøl – can substitute any caffeine and alcohol-free malted type beverage
- 1 tsp. of yeast, fresh

Instructions:

1. Add water, lemon juice and sugar to large pot. Bring to boil.

2. Once water is boiling, remove from heat. Let it cool for about an hour.

3. Add in vørterøl or substitute and the fresh yeast. Stir thoroughly till yeast is dissolved. Allow mixture to set for eight hours without refrigeration.

4. Serve. Store snarøl in refrigerator. It will be slightly carbonated, but not alcoholic.

15 – Beef & Cabbage

Beef is second only to lamb and game meat in consumption among Norwegians. The beef is simmered with cabbage in the most popular way to prepare it.

Makes 6 Servings

Cooking + Prep Time: 2 hours & 20 minutes

Ingredients:

- 1 cabbage head, medium or large
- 4 to 5 lbs. of beef, boned or de-boned
- 2 cups of water, filtered
- Salt, kosher
- 4 tsp. of black pepper, whole

Instructions:

1. Rinse cabbage and cut it into large-sized wedges. Cut beef in large pieces.

2. Pour water in large sized pot.

3. Layer meat and cabbage in pot and salt between the layers. Begin and end with cabbage layers.

4. Add whole pepper to tea strainer to contain it. Place in pot with cabbage and meat.

5. Cover pot and bring to boil. Lower temperature to gentle boil. Add water as needed and don't allow pot to dry. Allow to cook for two to two and a half hours till meat is tender and easily pulled apart.

6. Pour meat stock over the beef and potatoes. Serve cabbage and meat with the potatoes boiled in water.

16 – Trout in Paper Wrappers

Trout is not the first fish people think of when they picture Norway, but it offers a taste like salmon without the high price. We eat this dish a lot during the summer months.

Makes 4 Servings

Cooking + Prep Time: 1/2 hour

Ingredients:

- 4 fillets, trout
- Salt, kosher, as desired
- 1/2 thin-sliced onion, red
- 1/2 thin-sliced lemon, fresh
- 4 tsp. of Cajun seasoning mix, sodium-free
- Oil, olive
- Butter, unsalted

Instructions:

1. Preheat the oven to 375F.

2. Place fillets individually in large squares of baking paper. Season as desired.

3. Arrange lemon and onions on the top. Divide evenly over fillets.

4. Top lemon and onion with Cajun seasoning. Top that with butter pat and a bit of oil.

5. Fold, then crimp baking paper tightly around edges in small-sized folds to make half-moon shapes. Press as you're crimping and seal packets well. You don't want steam escaping. Arrange packets on cookie sheet.

6. Bake fish for 13 to 15 minutes, till fish is thoroughly cooked and it flakes easily.

7. Cut packets open. Remove fish to plate. Dress with liquid in bags. Serve.

17 – Salmon & Matcha Spice

The salmon and matcha powder together make a great combination in this dish. The rub of matcha oil with spices can be made in advance, too, which will save time the day you make the fish.

Makes 4 Servings

Cooking + Prep Time: 70 minutes + 4 hours separation time

Ingredients:

- 1/2 cup + 4 tbsp. of matcha powder
- Salt, kosher
- 2 cups of oil, grape seed
- 1/2 cup of sesame seeds, raw white, ground
- 1 tsp. of ground pepper, WHITE
- 4 x 4-oz. pieces of salmon, Norwegian or locally sourced
- 1 tbsp. of julienned ginger, fresh
- 1 cup of peeled edamame
- 1 fresh lemon, zest and juice only
- 1 tbsp. of tamari
- 2 tbsp. of chopped chives
- Watercress

Instructions:

1. To prepare matcha oil, add a half-cup of the matcha powder and 1 pinch salt to dry sauté pan over med. heat. Mix and heat ingredients slowly till they smoke a bit.

2. Add and whisk in grape seed oil. Set aside. When cooled, transfer oil to glass jar. Set it aside. Allow jar to set for four hours, so ingredients can separate. Don't stir.

3. To prepare spice/matcha rub, mix remainder of matcha powder with sesame seeds, pinch of salt and the WHITE pepper on plate.

4. Place salmon in spice blend. Coat well. All sides should be coated.

5. In sauté pan, pour about 1 tbsp. of matcha oil for cooking fish. Add salmon. Cook for one minute for each side.

6. Remove salmon from pan. Allow it to rest.

7. Place the salmon on the watercress. Garnish with chives, tamari, lemon juice and zest, ginger and edamame. Serve.

18 – Baked Fish with Macaroni

This is a traditional Norwegian dish made with macaroni and baked fish. It's rather like mac and cheese with green peas and cod added.

Makes 4-6 Servings

Cooking + Prep Time: 50 minutes

Ingredients:

- 2 cups of macaroni
- 3 tbsp. of butter, unsalted
- 4 tbsp. of flour, all-purpose
- 1 & 1/2 cups of milk, 2%
- 1 cup of grated cheese
- 1/4 tsp. of ground nutmeg
- Salt, kosher, as desired
- Pepper, ground, as desired
- 1 & 1/4 pounds of uncooked cod fillet, de-boned, skinned, cubed
- 1 cup of green peas, fresh
- 1 cup of breadcrumbs, dried

Instructions:

1. Cook macaroni in large pot of water using package instructions. Drain and rinse with water. Set it aside.

2. Preheat oven to 390F.

3. Melt butter in pot. Once it's nearly melted, whisk in flour till it forms a paste. Allow paste to cook for one or two minutes. Add milk. Whisk till smooth. Cook for two to three minutes, till it starts to thicken a bit.

4. Place handful of cheese into sauce. Stir well. Allow cheese to melt a little, then stir and add more cheese. Continue working this way till all cheese has melted and has been incorporated well into smooth sauce.

5. Add nutmeg. Season as desired. Set mixture aside. Allow to cool for five minutes.

6. To assemble dish, add macaroni to baking dish. Layer in peas and cod. Pour cheese sauce on top. Sprinkle with breadcrumbs. Lastly, bake for about 25 to 30 minutes, till top is golden brown. Serve.

19 – Norwegian Curried Lamb

If you crave for the taste of lamb curry made like they do in Norway, or are curious to try it, this is an easy dish to make. Cooking it slowly, whether in a pot, as in this recipe, or a slow cooker, yields a tender and tasty dinner.

Makes 5 Servings

Cooking + Prep Time: 1 hour

Ingredients:

- 3 pounds of chunk-cut lamb
- 1/4 cup of flour, all-purpose
- 3 minced cloves of garlic
- 1 chopped onion, large
- 1 tsp. of salt, kosher
- 1 tsp. of pepper, ground
- 2 tbsp. of curry powder

For the browning sauce: margarine

Instructions:

1. Coat the meat with all-purpose flour. Sauté the onion and garlic in a bit of margarine. Heat more of the margarine in heavy skillet. Brown the meat on each side and transfer it to large sized pot.

2. Add sautéed garlic and onions to the pot. Season with curry power, kosher salt & ground pepper. Add a cup of hot water. Bring to boil. Then, add additional water as needed to cover the meat. Cover pot. Simmer till tender, 25-30 minutes. Check the seasonings. You want them strong. Serve while hot.

20 – Norwegian Lemon Chicken

This lemon chicken dish is delightful, plus it's easy and quick to make. The baked chicken benefits from a refreshing blend of seasonings and lemon.

Makes 4 Servings

Cooking + Prep Time: 1 hour & 25 minutes

Ingredients:

- 2 & 1/2 – 3 pounds of chicken
- 2 tbsp. of oil, olive
- 2 eggs, large
- 1 & 1/2 lemons, juice only
- 1 tbsp. of lemon zest, fresh
- 1 cup of broth, chicken, warmed

Optional: 1 tsp. of garlic powder

- 1 tbsp. of chopped parsley, fresh
- Salt, kosher, as desired
- Pepper, ground, as desired

Instructions:

1. Preheat the oven to 350F.

2. Flour, then lightly season chicken pieces.

3. Pour the oil in shallow pan that can be used to serve. Heat, then sauté the chicken on each side till golden in color.

4. Beat the eggs. Add the lemon juice and zest.

5. Whisk while gradually adding chicken broth.

6. Pour the mixture over chicken. Sprinkle parsley on top.

7. Bake chicken in 350F oven for 35-40 minutes and serve.

21 – Norwegian Saffron Salmon

The salmon in Norway have a rich flavor, not found anywhere else. In this dish, it is combined with a sauce made from fennel, saffron and butter. It's amazing.

Makes 4 Servings

Cooking + Prep Time: 1 hour & 10 minutes

Ingredients:

- 12 crushed threads of saffron
- 9 tbsp. of butter, unsalted
- 1/2 cup of fennel bulb, minced with reserved fronds
- 1 minced shallot, large
- 4 x 6-ounce salmon fillets, boneless, skinless
- Salt, kosher, as desired
- Pepper, ground, as desired
- 24 mussels
- 3 tbsp. of white vermouth, dry
- 1 cup of wine, white
- 1 tbsp. of minced chives, fresh
- 1 tbsp. of minced parsley leaves, fresh
- 1 tbsp. of minced tarragon leaves, fresh

Instructions:

1. Heat the oven to 225F.

2. Next, combine 1 & 1/2 cups of warm water with saffron in small-sized bowl and set it aside.

3. Grease a 10-inch skillet using a tbsp. of butter. Arrange the shallots and fennel at the bottom of the skillet. Season the salmon as desired and arrange it in the skillet.

4. Scatter the mussels around the fillets. Pour wine and extra saffron liquid around salmon. Cover. Bring to boil and reduce the heat to med-low. Cook till mussels open, usually three minutes or so. Remove the pan from heat. Cover it and set it aside. Allow it to steam till salmon has cooked through. Transfer fish and opened mussels to baking sheet. Place sheet in oven.

5. Return the skillet to high heat. Add the vermouth. Bring to boil. Add and whisk in remainder of butter, 1 tbsp. after another. Remove the pan from heat. Add and stir in tarragon, chives and parsley. Season the broth as desired.

6. Divide mussels and fish into four bowls. Spoon some broth over each. Garnish with fronds of fennel. Serve.

22 – Norway Salmon Chowder

Norwegian salmon chowder uses Atlantic salmon, which are quite easy to find in the cold waters around Norway. The salmon in your area will suffice, though. Add a salad and baguettes, and you have a filling and tasty dinner.

Makes 4 Servings

Cooking + Prep Time: 1 hour

Ingredients:

- 1 lb. fish fillet
- 6 or 7 cups of diced potatoes, redskin
- 1 cup of carrots, medium, chopped
- 1 cup of celery, chopped
- 1/3 cup of green and red peppers
- 1/3 cup of corn, frozen
- 1/3 cup of potatoes, instant
- 1/3 cup of fresh parsley, chopped
- 1/3 cup of onions, chopped
- 3 chopped garlic cloves

For garnishing: 1/3 cup of chives

- 3 cups of water, filtered
- 3 cups of milk, 2%
- 2 cups of cream, light
- 1 or 2 cubes of bouillon, fish
- 1 tbsp. of Worcestershire sauce, low sodium
- Salt, kosher, as desired
- Pepper, fresh ground, as desired

Instructions:

1. Sauté garlic and onions till they are transparent.

2. Place the water, bouillon cube, carrots, potatoes and kosher salt in soup kettle. Simmer for 13-15 minutes. Add rest of veggies. Simmer gently.

3. In separate medium bowl, whisk milk and instant potatoes. Stir while adding gradually.

4. Add the fish. Stir until the soup has thickened. Reduce heat. Crumble fish into smaller sized pieces when it cooks. Gradually add cream and stir.

5. Season with Worcestershire sauce, kosher salt and ground pepper, as desired. Turn off heat. Allow mixture to rest for several minutes. Garnish with chives and serve.

23 – Norwegian Spinach & Quinoa Salad

The light, bright flavors in this salad help you to fight off those cold-weather blues. It's packed with baby greens, spinach, quinoa, pomegranate seeds, mangos and Feta cheese. It's a high-protein light dinner or lunch.

Makes 5 Servings

Cooking + Prep Time: 35 minutes

Ingredients:

- 1/2 cup of oil, olive
- 1/3 cup of vinegar, white balsamic
- 2 tbsp. of water, filtered
- 1/2 tsp. of salt, sea
- 1/4 tsp. of pepper, ground
- 1/2 tsp. of honey, pure
- 3/4 lb. of peeled shrimp
- 6 oz. of spinach, baby
- 4 oz. of salad greens, mixed
- 2 peeled, diced whole mangoes, large
- 1 & 1/4 cup of pomegranate seeds
- 1 cup of cooked quinoa
- 1 cup of chopped walnuts
- 1/3 cup of cheese, feta

Instructions:

1. In food processor, combine oil, vinegar, water, salt, ground pepper and pure honey. Blend till creamy and smooth and set it aside.

2. In large sized pan, add 2 tbsp. of dressing prepared in step 1. Heat on med-high till hot. Add the shrimp and cook till cooked through and pink on each side. Set them aside.

3. In large sized bowl, combine mixed greens, baby spinach, pomegranate seeds, mangoes, walnuts, quinoa, cooked shrimp and feta cheese. Drizzle dressing over top. Toss and combine well. Serve.

24 – Stewed Peas

Peas are healthy legumes, and Norwegian cooks make this as a side dish for lamb, pork, roast beef or meatballs. It's as nutritious as it is delicious.

Makes 2-3 Servings

Cooking + Prep Time: 1/2 hour

Ingredients:

- 2 cups of green peas, split, dried
- Water, filtered, as needed
- Sugar, granulated, as desired
- Butter, unsalted, as desired
- 1 tsp. of salt, kosher

Instructions:

1. Place the peas in a pan. Cover them with filtered water. Add 1 tsp. of kosher salt.

2. Bring to a boil. Turn down heat and simmer.

3. Cover pan. Cook till softened. Add water as needed.

4. Stir, then mash the peas. Add sugar and butter as desired. Serve.

25 – Norwegian Leeks & Tuna Pasta

This easy dinner is one you can make mostly from ingredients you already have at home. It lets you spend less time on meal prep and more time enjoying the delicious meal with family and friends.

Makes 4 Servings

Cooking + Prep Time: 65 minutes

Ingredients:

- 1 leek, medium
- 1 can of water-packed tuna
- 2 cups of penne pasta, dry
- 7 ounces of cream cheese, light
- 1/2 cup of milk, 2%
- 1/2 cup of water, hot
- 2 tbsp. of Parmesan, grated
- 1 piece of cheese, your choice
- Oregano
- Basil
- Salt, kosher
- Pepper, WHITE

Instructions:

1. Preheat oven to 400F.

2. Open tuna. Drain. Discard liquid. Place in dish you'll use to make the dinner. Crush with fork. Add chopped leek, creamed cheese, salt, pepper & herbs. Mix thoroughly.

3. Add the uncooked pasta. Mix and cover all pieces of pasta. Add milk and water. Grate cheese. Sprinkle over the top. Bake for 45 minutes and serve.

Norway is home to a diverse array of dessert choices. Try one of these wonderful desserts soon...

26 – Rice & Date Pudding

This rice pudding has been served by grandmothers in Norway during the Christmas season for many years. It's a holiday favorite.

Makes 8 Servings

Cooking + Prep Time: 45 minutes + 3 hours chilling time

Ingredients:

- 1/2 cup of water, cold
- 2 tbsp. of rice, uncooked
- 1 cup of whipping cream
- 20 pitted, chopped dates
- 1/2 cup of sugar, powdered
- 1 x 1/4-oz. envelope of gelatin, unflavored
- 1/4 cup of water, filtered
- 1/2 tsp. of vanilla extract, pure

Instructions:

1. In medium pan, bring the water to boil. Add rice. Stir. Reduce the heat and cover pan. Simmer for 15-20 minutes. When rice is cooked, drain off excess water, if any, then spread on plate and allow to cool.

2. Whip cream till stiff. Add and stir in cooled rice, dates & confectioner's sugar. Then sprinkle gelatin over water surface. Set over pot of boiling, filtered water till it dissolves. Stir this into the rice mixture. Add vanilla.

3. Place bowl in refrigerator. Chill till mixture starts thickening. Once rice doesn't settle to bottom anymore, rinse a mold, moistening inside. Pour rice mixture in. Chill till it sets, three hours or so. Remove from mold. Serve when cold.

27 – Cinnamon Thumbs

These buttery, sweet cookies almost melt in your mouth when you eat them. The texture and flavor are similar to that of shortbread cookies, with cinnamon and sugar.

Makes 4-5 dozen Servings

Cooking + Prep Time: 25 minutes

Ingredients:

For cookies

- 1 cup of butter, unsalted
- 5 tbsp. of sugar, granulated
- 2 cups of flour, all-purpose
- 1 tsp. of vanilla, pure

To roll

- 1/4 cup of sugar, granulated
- 1 tsp. of cinnamon, ground

Instructions:

1. Preheat oven to 350F.

2. Beat butter and sugar together till fluffy. Add vanilla and flour. Beat till you have a dough. Roll dough balls into skinny, long ropes. Cut dough in 2-inch pieces, diagonally.

3. Place the cookies several inches apart on lined cookie sheet. Bake for 8 to 10 minutes till bottom edges start turning golden. Remove from oven. Allow cookies to cool a bit.

4. As cookies cool, combine sugar and cinnamon in bowl. When you can handle cookies, roll them gently in cinnamon/sugar mixture. Place on cooling rack and let them finish cooling. Serve.

28 – Norwegian Spiced Krumkake

This recipe is one of the most traditional Krumkake recipes you'll find. Be sure not to skip adding the cardamom or the orange rind and zest. They make the cake special.

Makes 30 cookies

Cooking + Prep Time: 55 minutes

Ingredients:

- 1 cup of sugar, white
- 1/2 cup of softened butter, unsalted
- 2 eggs, medium
- 1 tsp. of zest, orange
- 1/4 tsp. of cloves, ground
- 1/4 tsp. of cardamom, ground
- 1 & 1/2 cups of flour, all-purpose
- 1 cup of milk, 2%

Instructions:

1. In medium-sized bowl, cream butter, orange peel, eggs and sugar together. Sift flour, cardamom and cloves together.

2. Next, add the dry ingredients to creamed mixture and alternate additions with milk. Mix till the batter is fully smooth.

3. Grease krumkake or waffle iron with veggie spray or oil. Turn heat to med-low.

4. Place 1 tbsp. batter after another into middle of iron. Close and hold it shut. Cook for 15-20 seconds, turning the iron over when halfway done. Remove the krumkake from the iron. Roll them into cones. Repeat with remainder of batter and serve.

29 – Norwegian Apple Cake

Some people are less than thrilled when they think of apples and cake together. But you'll actually be spoiling your family with this apple cake, and I bet they'll love it.

Makes 6 Servings

Cooking + Prep Time: 50 minutes

Ingredients:

- 4 & 1/2 oz. of melted butter, unsalted
- 4 & 1/2 oz. of sugar, granulated
- 2 eggs, large
- 1 tbsp. of vanilla extract, pure
- 4 oz. of flour, all-purpose
- 1 tsp. of baking powder, sodium free
- 2 tbsp. of milk, 2%
- 1 apple, large
- 1 tsp. of cinnamon, ground
- 1 tbsp. of sugar, demerara

Instructions:

1. Preheat the oven to 400F.

2. Grease, then flour 8" cake pan. Set aside.

3. Combine baking powder and flour in small bowl. Set it aside.

4. In bowl of stand mixer with whisk, cream butter and sugar till fluffy and light, with sugar dissolved.

5. Add eggs one after another and mix well after each one is added. Add vanilla extract.

6. Add all milk and 1/2 flour mixture.

7. Mix well. Add rest of flour mixture. Combine till there are no remaining flour streaks.

8. Spread batter in pan prepared above.

9. Core, then halve the apple. Slice halves into 1/8-inch slices. Arrange atop batter. Sprinkle with demerara sugar and cinnamon.

10. Bake for 35 minutes till golden brown in color. Serve warm.

30 – Kringla Cookies

There are numerous recipes for Kringla cookies in Norway, and this is one of the best. It uses sour cream instead of buttermilk, which adds a unique taste.

Makes 24 cookies

Cooking + Prep Time: 1 hour & 10 minutes + 8-12 hours refrigeration time

Ingredients:

- 1 cup of cream, heavy
- 1 x 8-oz. container of sour cream, light
- 1 & 1/3 cups of sugar, white
- 2 tbsp. of shortening
- 3 cups of flour, all-purpose
- 1 yolk from large egg
- 2 tsp. of baking powder, low sodium
- 1 tsp. of baking soda, gluten-free
- 1 tsp. of vanilla extract, pure

Instructions:

1. In small-sized bowl, stir cream and sour cream together. Cover. Place in the refrigerator and leave it there overnight.

2. Allow sour cream mixture to come back to room temp. Preheat oven to 475F.

3. In large-sized bowl, mix egg yolk, sugar and shortening together. Stir baking soda and vanilla into sour cream mixture. Stir that mixture into bowl with shortening and sugar till blended well. Combine baking powder and flour. Stir into batter till incorporated fully.

4. Place dough on floured work surface. Make dough balls the size of ping pong balls. Roll into 8-9" ropes. Form into lazy eight signs. Pinch ends together. Place on cookie sheets.

5. Bake for five minutes in 475F oven till slightly browned. Completely cool before you serve.

Conclusion

This Norwegian cookbook has shown you…

How to use different ingredients to affect unique Scandinavian tastes in dishes both well-known and rare.

How can you include the tastes of Norway in your home recipes?

You can…

- Make Norwegian meatballs, which I imagine everyone knows about. They are just as tasty as you have heard.
- Learn to cook with lingonberries, which are widely used in Norway. Find it in a jam at ethnic or European type food markets.
- Enjoy making the delectable seafood dishes of Norway, including salmon, mackerel and cod. Fish is a mainstay in the region, and there are SO many ways to make it great.
- Make dishes using asparagus and sweet peas, which are often used in Nordic cooking.
- Make various types of desserts, like Norwegian cookies and apple cakes, that will tempt your family's sweet tooth.

Have fun experimenting! Enjoy the results!

About the Author

Allie Allen developed her passion for the culinary arts at the tender age of five when she would help her mother cook for their large family of 8. Even back then, her family knew this would be more than a hobby for the young Allie and when she graduated from high school, she applied to cooking school in London. It had always been a dream of the young chef to study with some of Europe's best and she made it happen by attending the Chef Academy of London.

After graduation, Allie decided to bring her skills back to North America and open up her own restaurant. After 10 successful years as head chef and owner, she decided to sell her business and pursue other career avenues. This monumental decision led Allie to her true calling, teaching. She also started to write e-books for her students to study at home for practice. She is now the proud author of several e-books and gives private and semi-private cooking lessons to a range of students at all levels of experience.

Stay tuned for more from this dynamic chef and teacher when she releases more informative e-books on cooking and baking in the near future. Her work is infused with stores and anecdotes you will love!

Author's Afterthoughts

I can't tell you how grateful I am that you decided to read my book. My most heartfelt thanks that you took time out of your life to choose my work and I hope you find benefit within these pages.

There are so many books available today that offer similar content so that makes it even more humbling that you decided to buying mine.

Tell me what you thought! I am eager to hear your opinion and ideas on what you read as are others who are looking for a good book to buy. Leave a review on Amazon.com so others can benefit from your wisdom!

With much thanks,

Allie Allen

Printed in Great Britain
by Amazon

82505747R00047